AF283099

Dear
Santa Claws
Cats' Letters to Santa

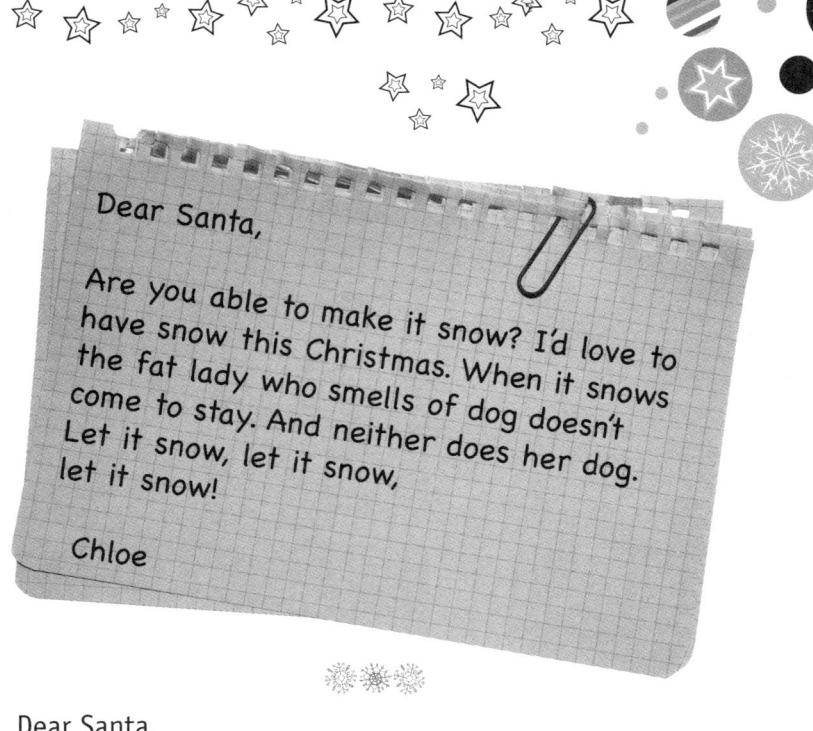

Dear Santa,

Are you able to make it snow? I'd love to have snow this Christmas. When it snows the fat lady who smells of dog doesn't come to stay. And neither does her dog. Let it snow, let it snow, let it snow!

Chloe

Dear Santa,

Would you be able to arrange a house swap? I live in an old ruin in Rome, which is very popular with tourists and has a thriving social scene. I'm prepared to trade places with a cat from a nice quiet villa in Tuscany. I think it would be interesting for both of us to experience a different lifestyle, don't you?

Ciao,

Gato

Dear Santa,

I'm desperate to get hold of a copy of *Recognizing Garden Birds* by PB Wellington. I've been picking bits of shuttlecock out of my teeth for weeks now.

Mr T

Dear Santa,

Is it ok to ask for two presents?
I could really do with a chalkboard and
some chalk so I can keep count of my
lives. I've got a horrible feeling I'm
getting close to nine.

Yours somewhat gloomily,
    Dante

Dear Santa,

All I'm hoping for this Christmas is peace, love and Chunky Chicken Chunks. What's so funny about that?

May the horse of harmony help to pull your sleigh,
Daffodil

Dear Santa,

I've arranged for a photographer to take a picture of my grandchildren all together. It's not often you get them all in one place and I'm very excited about the results. However, I'll need a frame for it. About 4 inches high by, say, 60 inches wide should do it. Can you oblige?

Tom

Dear Santa,

Please can I have a new lucky dip? The one my owner gives me doesn't seem to have any toys left in it, only my own 'doings'.

Love,

    Barnum

Dear Santa,

Simple request: some air-freshener please. My people don't seem to mind the pong, but I do!

Yours sweetly,
    Desiree

Dear Santa,

I know this is a bit extravagant, but I would really love a reel-to-reel tape machine. Milton at No. 47 has got one and it keeps him amused for hours, watching those reels go round and round. And he says it keeps him fit.

Best wishes,
  Dizzy

PS: One with a volume control, so it doesn't make that awful noise.

Dear Santa,

This is my first Christmas and I think I've outgrown my litter tray. Please could you bring me one of those attractive indoor bonsai tree gardens? Much more fun.

Thanks in anticipation,
Fluffy Dumpling

Dear Santa,

Christmas already? Goodness, how time flies while one's sleeping. Well, it'll have to be the usual again I suppose. Can I try the white chocolate ones this time, though?

Much obliged,
   Oscar

Dear Santa,

I was recently taken to see a smiling lady who made me go to sleep. That's no great feat in itself, but when I woke up I found she'd cut me open and put a tiny electronic chip under my skin. The impertinence of it! Apparently this chip tells people what my name is and where I live, although I keep pressing it and no sound comes out at all. I'm assured it works for humans. Which led me to thinking: if they can make a chip that tells people who I am and where I live, how about one that tells them what I like to eat. Or, more specifically, that I DON'T LIKE LIVER. I'm not just any old cat, you know.

Ta-ta,

Claude

Dear Santa,

Have you ever thought of giving the reindeer a year off and getting your sleigh pulled by dogs? I'm sure reindeer do an excellent job, but wouldn't you find it more fun whipping dogs? I know I would.

Happy Christmas,

Kiki

Dear Santa,

I'm planning a trip away with the owl from No.18 (I think she fancies me). We'll be needing supplies: honey, money, that sort of stuff. Oh, and a boat, preferably pea green.

Best wishes,

Pussy

Dear Santa,

My cousin Vita has taken to sending out those form letters at Christmas, updating everyone on what all her kittens have been up to. I find this somewhat impersonal, not to mention tedious. She's 21 years old and has 47 children. Mind you, a couple of them are clearly going off the rails, which I find rather amusing. Help me get into the Christmas spirit, will you, Santa?

Fiddlesticks

Dear Santa,

Is there a car seat for cats? If so, I'd like one please. I don't see why that screaming brat should get to ride up front while I'm crammed into a cage on the parcel shelf.

Ginger

Dear Santa,

About six months ago the little boy who shares my bed came home with a net on a stick. He put it in the corner of the room and never uses it, but he won't let me have it either. So I would really like one of my own please. He may not know what to do with it but I sure do. I hope you can make my wish come true. It would mean a week of fish suppers and I wouldn't even get my paws wet.

FOXY

Dear Santa,

Bit of a long shot, but I don't suppose the power of speech would be within your capabilities, would it? I've lost faith in body language. My people seem to think that me lying comatose with my legs outstretched is a request to have my tummy tickled. What do they think I am, a dog? How can I get the message across that it means 'SLEEPING – DO NOT DISTURB' without actually telling them in plain English? Can you help? Just a few words would do.

Yours more in hope than expectation,

Martin

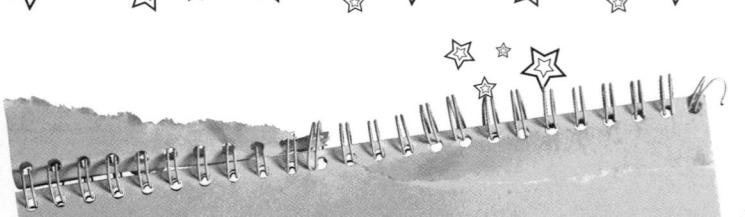

Dear Santa,

Panto season is upon us and once again I suppose I'll be overlooked for the role of Puss In Boots. In this day and age you would think they'd give a cat role to an actual cat, wouldn't you? Last year I auditioned to play the cat in the local amateur dramatic society's performance of Dick Whittington. I was the only cat that tried out for the part but guess what: they gave it to that idiot dog walker from No.105, whose range of acting skills extends to licking her imaginary paw and doing an abysmal miaow. To give her her due, she did give a remarkably convincing portrayal of a hippopotamus.

Sorry to burden you with all this, Santa. Please don't think I'm bitter.

Yours,
   Olivier (a frustrated thespian)

PS: I hear all the parts in Cats are currently taken by humans.

Dear Santa,

I've been told I'm overweight. At 18 years old, I'd say this news has come a bit late in the day, but if you fancy bringing me one of those cat gyms, I'll give it a go. No weights though; I'm not pumping iron at my age.

Benny

Dear Santa,

Please can you bring me a small pump and fountain that will fit into my water bowl. There's something about that still water – I just can't get excited about it.

Thank you,

Cleo

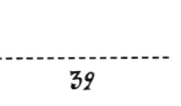

Dear Santa,

I would really really like to have my own personal flag, so that when I get to the top of the curtains I can unfurl it and show all the other cats that I got there first. I saw someone do this on top of a mountain, and I'm told they also did it on the moon – yeah right, like the moon's a place. I'll leave the design to you: something with a picture of me on it looking heroic and perhaps some dead mice here and there.

Onwards and upwards,
    Scotty

Dear Santa,

I've been trying really hard to be good all year but accidents will happen. Some things are just unavoidable. So please can you bring me a Ming vase, a crystal decanter and another original of 'Sunflowers' by Vincent Van Gogh?

It wasn't my fault,
    Tyson

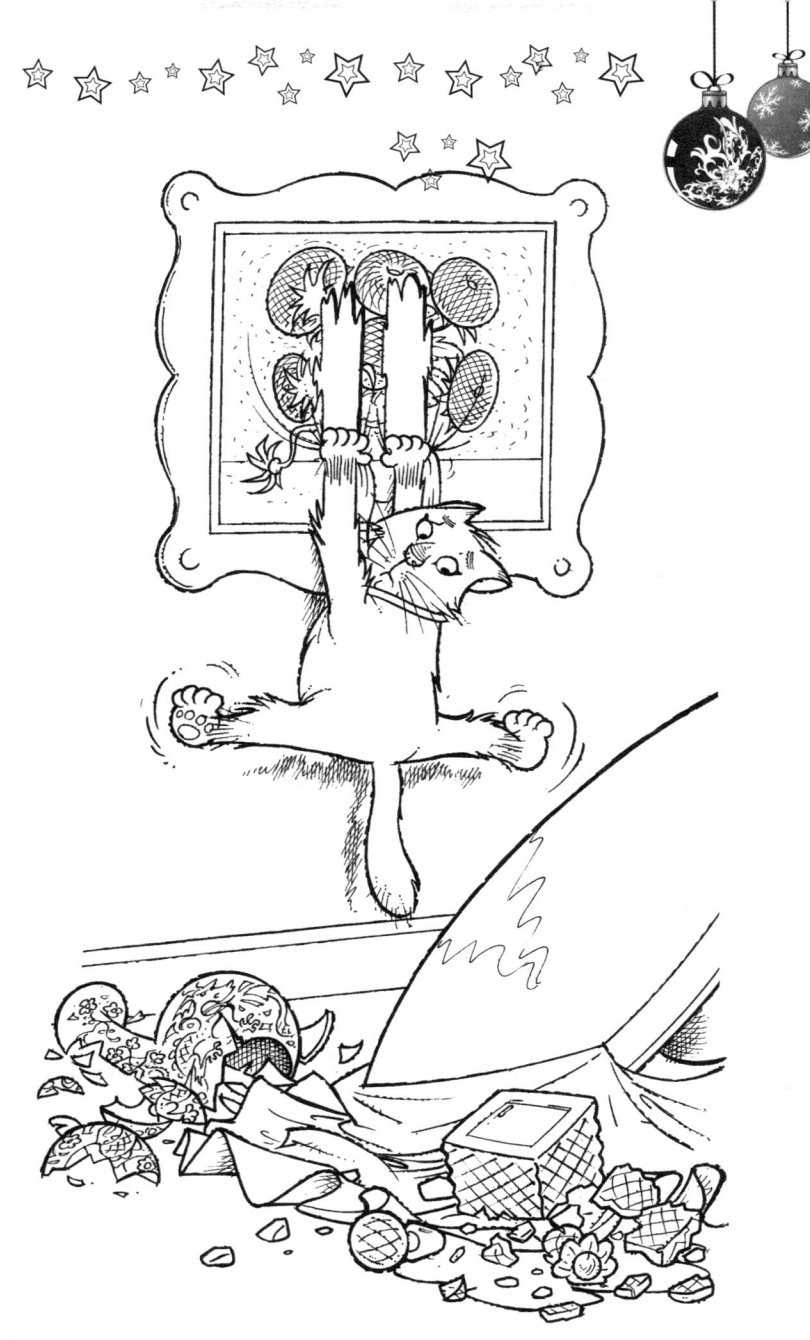

Dear Santa,

I heard a vicious rumour: a dog is for life, not just for Christmas. Say it ain't so, Santa, say it ain't so.

Marmalade

Dear Santa,

The little boy who eats my Cornflakes in the morning needs setting straight. Today I heard him saying that you don't exist. Hah! If that's the case, I thought to myself, where does he think I came from?

Miracle

Dear Santa,

I've been searching through the catalogues for something that makes a meow travel through glass. When I tell my idiot owners that it's time to let me in, they just look at me through the window and laugh. My sister Phoebe says it's cos I look comical making all the meow faces. For crying out loud! Well, if only.

Domingo

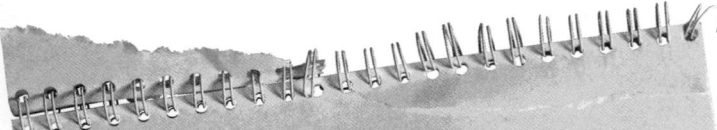

Dear Santa,

Can you get paw extensions? The hole in the lid of the fish tank is too narrow for me to get my whole arm through beyond the elbow, so I need about another three inches if I'm to get the darned fish out of there. I know that's what I'm supposed to do, and it's not for want of trying.

Yours in exasperation,

Molly

Dear Santa,

Could you please bring me a miniature person that I can pick up and tickle whenever I feel the urge, even when they're asleep.

See how they like it.

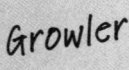
Growler

Dear Santa,

Do they make computer games for cats? I think they must do because I keep hearing the little boy who wears my socks saying something about a 'paws button', but I can't seem to make it work. Please look into it.

Thanks,

Mario

Dear Santa,

Do you have a cat? Would you like one? Is there room on your sleigh? I'll be waiting by the fireplace.

Houdini

PS: I may have eaten the mince pies.

Dear Santa,

I've always wondered why they put my address tag on a collar round my neck where I can't read it. What are they trying to do, torture me? Is there anything you can do about this? A mirror perhaps? Or some kind of CatNav?

I would be grateful,

    Scatty

Dear Santa,

It's been a bit of a miserable year for everyone in this house, what with the arrival of the new puppy and everything. We could do with some music to lighten the mood, preferably something I can sing along to, like Alanis Morrissette or Whitney Houston.

Yours in music,

Screecher

Dear Santa,

Groucho Marx once said, and I quote: 'Time flies like an arrow; fruit flies like a banana.' I'm intrigued. Please can I have a flying banana?

Thank you,
 Tarby

Dear Santa,

I'm in need of inspiration. Please can you bring me a book of quotations from Chairman Miaow. Serve the felines!

Sasha

Dear Santa,

Why was I left out when the fur coats were being handed out? I know we can't all be beautiful, but why me? I'm as cute as any other cat on the inside. And what's with the enormous ears? Is it because I'm Mexican? Is that what this is all about? Well, I don't think it's funny. Come on, a joke's a joke, but I think it's time you handed over my mink.

Juanita

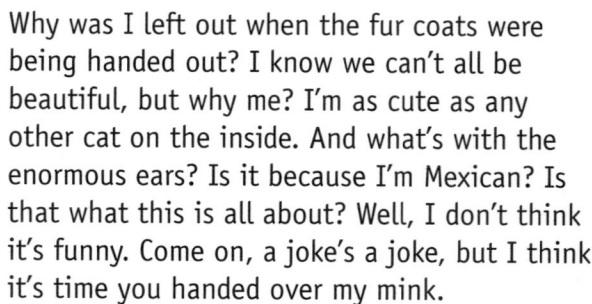

Dear Santa,

Can you arrange it for me to spend a day inside the mind of a dog? It would be so fascinating to discover what's going on in there.

Sigmund

PS: Just for one day, mind.

Dear Santa,

There's something I've been trying to get hold of for ages and I've just found out the name of it: tin opener. I'd be eternally grateful if you could bring me a tin opener. Oh, and the instruction manual too please.

Yours,
    Gilbert

Dear Santa,

This year I've learnt to climb, prowl, jump and mew in a way that makes hardened scaffolders go `aah'. Next year I'm thinking of learning a second language, probably squirrel or sparrow. Please could you bring me the relevant reading matter?

Sincerely yours,
   Einstein

LEARN FLUENT
SPARROW
IN 3 WEEKS

Dear Santa,

I wonder if you could clear up an argument I've been having with Tiddles from over the back. He reckons that if you go beyond the fence at number 73 you fall off the edge of the world. I, on the other hand, have a theory that the world is round, and if you jump the fence at number 73 you will land in the vegetable patch at number 5. But I haven't plucked up the courage to try it. Could you shed any light on the matter before I embark on a voyage that could spell certain death?

Your humble servant,

Columbus

Dear Santa,

I'm only writing to you for old times'
sake. When you get to my age, there's
nothing you really want, and no point
asking for anything longlasting as I
probably won't be around to enjoy it
for long. A box of tissues perhaps —
they're always fun for the little ones.
Or some Chocolate Mice. At 17, I think I
should be allowed the odd indulgence.

Yours,
    Croesus

Dear Santa,

I think it's time for a new set of fluffy white bathroom towels. I've pretty much sucked the last lot to death. And they're certainly not white any more.

Happy Christmas,

Pumpkin

Dear Santa,

Hmm, I know what you're thinking: what do you give the cat who has everything? Surprise me.

Suki Sugar Icing

Dear Santa,

Please can you bring me one of those amusing duck whistles? I've tried getting close to the birds in my garden but 'miaow' and 'hiss' just seem to scare them off. I need to communicate with them in terms they can understand. Oh, and one of those camouflage-pattern hats would be nice too.

Hemingway

Dear Santa,

This is a bit embarrassing. I am writing to you in strict confidence to ask if you can bring me a – I can hardly bring myself to say it – a hairpiece. I fell asleep yesterday and woke up to find an unsightly bald patch just in front of my left leg. Mortifying isn't the word. I've no idea how it got there but I'm desperate to cover it up. I can't go out in public and it's destroyed my libido. Please help.

Kitty

Dear Santa,

Same request as last year: please can you bring me some whisker extensions? Either these things are getting shorter or I'm getting wider.

Have a splendid Christmas,
   Boris

70

Dear Santa,

Ah, Christmas — a time for lying by the fire
with an endless supply of delicious nibbles and
a good book, watching with amusement while
the rest of the household rush around getting
stressed over an oversized chicken. A copy of
Old Possum's Book of Practical Humans by
S Toilet would fit the bill nicely, if you'd be so
kind, old chap.

All the best,
    Whisky

Dear Santa,

For Christmas I would very much like a book or video on how to do karate. I keep getting mauled by the Ukrainian Levkoy at No. 37 and my mum says it's time I learned to defend myself. A good working knowledge of the martial arts would see off that bullying Russki, she says, and make me more confident around girls into the bargain.

Yours sincerely,

Bob

Dear Santa,

I expect you heard about the vase. Is it worth me going any further with this letter?

Yours remorsefully,
   Wolfgang

PS: If it is, can I have my tail back? It seems to have affected my balance.

Dear Santa,

Can I have a bag of quicksand for my litter tray? I'm not the best at burying and it always takes so long.

Yours,
   Samson

Dear Santa,

Last year you overlooked my present. I know I only arrived here on Christmas morning but I thought you, of all people, would have known I was coming. Anyway, no excuses this year. I´ll be watching from the tree.

Mildred

Dear Santa,

I've been getting tired of my boring old collar and wanting to give it some bling. The dog's got one with studs in it, which is a bit butch if you ask me, but each to their own. I was thinking of something more glamorous. And then it struck me: a charm collar! Instead of just having that drab metal disc, you could adorn it with all sorts of darling things: a little bell, some string, a pen top, a dead mouse... the list is endless.

Food for thought,
    Coco

Dear Santa,

How about some of that colourful gravel the goldfish gets? My gravel's all grey and dull. If I had the colourful gravel I might take a bit more pride in keeping it nice.

Jenny

Dear Santa,

For Christmas, please can I have a goldfish?
Don't worry, I have my own bowl ;-)

Innocently yours,

Collis

Dear Santa,

Please can you bring me a copy of
Garfield The Movie? My mum won't let
me go out and watch it because she
thinks it'll lead me astray. If I had my
own copy I could sneak a look at it
while she's out mousing. Go on,
Santa. You know me – I'm not the
straying kind.

Please.

Pickles

Dear Santa,

I love climbing trees, me. You ask anyone, I'm the best tree climber in town. As soon as they let me out of the house in the morning, I'm up that willow tree like a rat up a drainpipe. Believe me, I'm the climbiest cat there is. I'm Climb-ey Fisher. I'm Climb-ate Change. I'm the thrilling Climb-max. For Christmas, please can you bring me a copy of *Talk Yourself Down* by Isaac M. Manx.

Thanks a million,
    Hillary

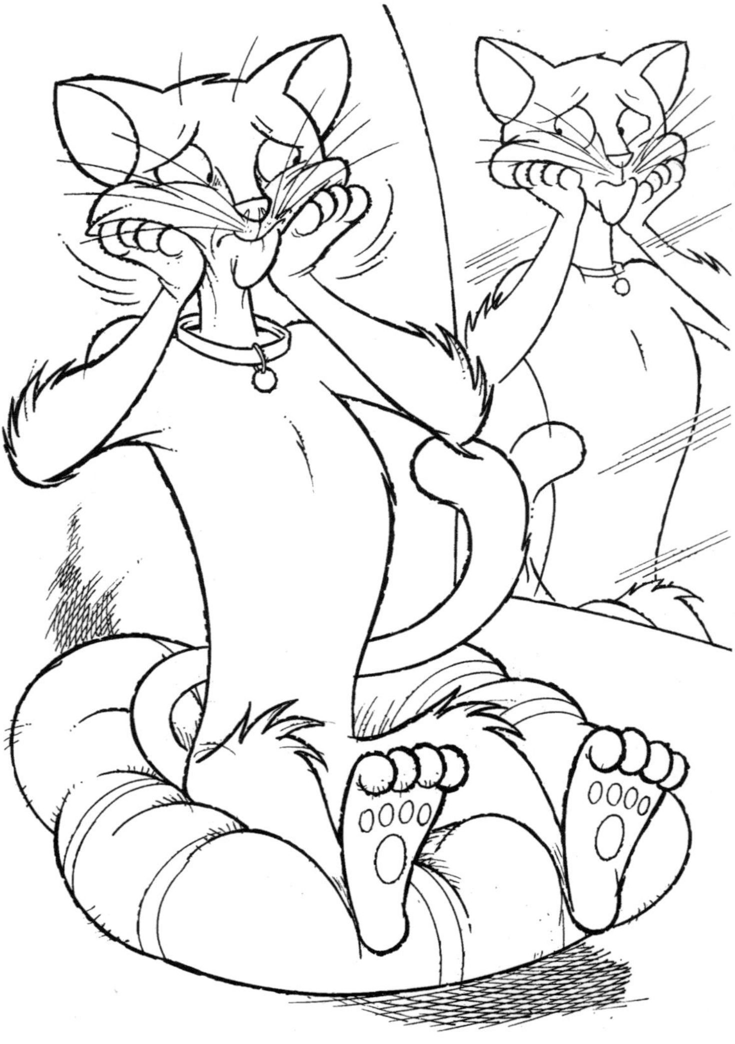

Dear Santa,

For Christmas I would dearly love some vouchers for Cuties Private Clinic. I'm worried that my fur makes my face look fat and I want it reduced. According to Coco it's because I'm a British Shorthair and she's an American Shorthair and my fur's just thicker than hers, but I don't see why I should have to live with the face I was born with if it makes me miserable. I tell you, she wouldn't – not for a minute.

I'm not asking for too much, am I, Sweetie?

Zaza

Dear Santa,

I don't suppose you've got room on your sleigh for a summerhouse, have you? Nothing too big, mind – not so big a human could get in it. I don't mind getting shoved out in the garden in the morning, but it would be less of an imposition if I had somewhere warm to go and lie down. Somewhere dry, with a nice warm rug and perhaps a real fire. And a door I can lock.

Warm regards,
Bullet

Dear Santa,

Please can you bring me an air horn for Christmas? When I was a kitten my owner thought it would be a good idea to train me to come running every time she tapped my dinner bowl. Pavlovian response, I believe it's called. Of course, now whenever I hear any little chink-chink sound I go running indoors expecting to find a tasty treat waiting for me. I've lost count of the times I've skidded to a halt in the kitchen, only to find it was just the milkman, or the batty woman next door putting her gin bottles out. It's making a dog of me. I was talking about this to my friend Claude, and he put his claw right on the nub of the problem. 'What you need,' he purred, 'is something distinctive, like a dinner gong.' Of course, Claude has a dinner gong. So, air horn please.

Much obliged,
Maxime

Dear Santa,

I hope you're well and looking forward to Christmas. I am. If you think I deserve it, I would really like one of those lovely ornate birdbaths, to add some interest to the garden, you understand. I've read that the best place to put them is just outside the kitchen window, within easy reach of the worktop.

All good wishes,
    Carnegie

Dear Santa,

I am writing to you not to ask for anything for myself, but in the hope that you will bestow a precious gift on the people I live with. And that is the gift of gratitude. Don't get me wrong, they're not bad people: they give me food and water and open the door for me, but whenever I bring them something from the garden, do they thank me? Do they heck! It doesn't hurt to express a bit of gratitude but I fear perhaps they know not how. Please help. Christmas with these people is a pitiful experience.

Sincerely yours,
   Rasputin

Dear Santa,

Can you do magic? I would love it if, just once, you could put the people who share my house under a spell during breakfast, so I can go around drinking the milk out of their cereal bowls, licking the butter and eating the jam to my heart's content, without getting shoved off the table all the time. Just for once. Well, once a month. Or week. Whatever you can do.

Hmm,

    Bernard

Dear Santa,
Is it within your powers to give me a train ticket to London? I've been reading about Dick Whittington, and it strikes me as a fine adventure, but I'm damned if I'm going to walk all that way.

Yours,
Eccles

Dear Santa,

I know I've missed Hallowe'en, but could you bring my mistress a new broomstick? I'm getting splinters.

Lucifer

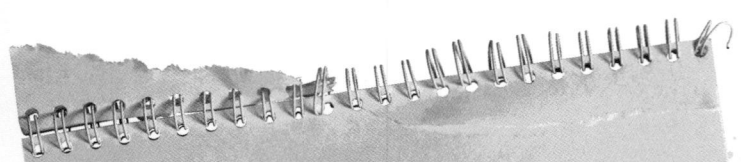

Dear Mr Christmas,

Would you be so kind as to bring the people who share my house a copy of *The Illustrated Anatomy of Cats* by Charles Spade. I think it's the only way they're going to get it into their heads that I'm a lady and change my name accordingly.

Yours,

Dave

Dear Santa,

I know I'm lucky that I'm not an `only cat', and Zebedee is an affectionate playmate, if a bit jumpy. But he has an unnatural tendency to gather fluff. Seriously, every time I lick his fur I end up with a mouth like the inside of a Hoover bag. So please can I have one of those defluffers for Christmas, so I can give him a once over before getting down to the affectionate stuff?

Yours truly,
Muffin

Dear Santa,

I've been watching the hamster a lot recently. He's an interesting little fellow. He's got this wheel in his cage which allows him to get some exercise without having to go anywhere. The people here have a bicycle in their bedroom that does the same. Do they make anything similar for cats? I feel disinclined to go outdoors when there's an 'r' in the month.

Best wishes of the season,

Dahlia

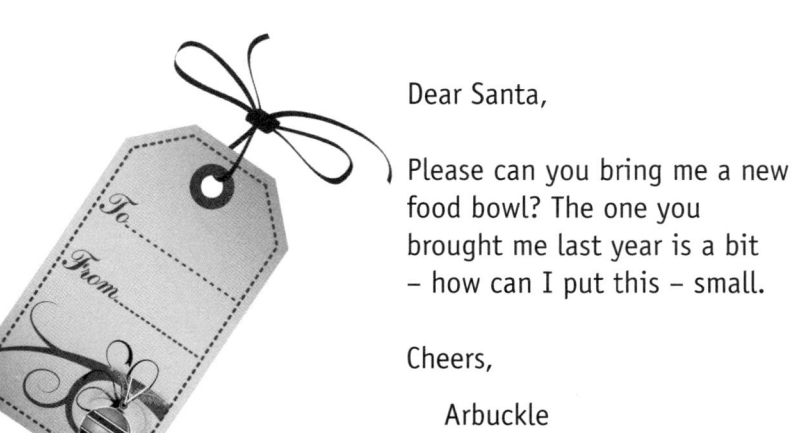

Dear Santa,

Please can you bring me a new food bowl? The one you brought me last year is a bit – how can I put this – small.

Cheers,

Arbuckle

Dear Santa,

You've no doubt heard that ridiculous joke that we cats are more interested in the paper our presents are wrapped in than the present itself. I don't expect for a second that you take that sort of nonsense seriously, but in case you were thinking of just bringing me a ball of wrapping paper, I thought I ought to write and point out there are much better presents for a cat. A diamond-encrusted collar, for example.

Miaow,

Mavis

Dear Santa,

I heard the neighbours whispering the other day about how my 'batty old' owner has me down to inherit her entire estate. Last year my ex-friend Anoushka from No. 65 inherited a fortune and wasted no time in moving out of the area into a full service cats' home overlooking a chicken farm. I know I shouldn't get excited by this sort of stuff, but I wonder if you could bring me a few innocent-looking balloons, inflated and ready to pop.

Yours in eager anticipation,

Crispin

Dear Santa,

Bernard the St Bernard from three doors down wears a miniature barrel round his neck, which I'm told is full of brandy. He says it's for his owner, in case he gets stuck up on a mountain, but his owner's a hairdresser from Brighton and, what's more, I've seen Bernard staggering home late at night with his owner having to hold on tight to keep him upright. I'm not saying I want to go the same way as Bernard, the poor mutt, but the idea of carrying your own sustenance around strikes me as rather ingenious. How about a nice little carton of fresh cream that hooks on to my collar, and maybe a straw?

Best wishes,
Jake

Dear Santa,

I would like for Christmas a deep-sea
diving suit for a cat. And one of those
little net bags they use for putting
things in, like fish and stuff.

Thank you,
Bubbles

Dear Santa,

I wonder what would happen if a nice book on Egyptology were to land on the hearth rug on Christmas morning and fall open on the bit about cat worship. Perhaps they'd get the message. I've been trying to drop subtle hints by building pyramids in my litter tray and scratching hieroglyphics in the kitchen table but I think they need something more explicit.

Bastet (that's not my real name)

Dear Santa,

I know you'll think this is an odd
request, but I've decided this house
needs a new dog. I miss the banter.

Happy Christmas,
    Jethro

Dear Santa,

Isn't the Internet a wonderful thing! I've been doing some surfing and I've discovered I'm supposed to be a magical creature with bewitching powers. How priceless! What do you think a 'magical creature' should ask for for Christmas? Potions and whatnot? Maybe some moondust? I'll try anything once.

   Chesney

Dear Santa,

Please can you bring me one of those flying suits – the ones humans use for xtreme base jumping? I assume they make them for cats. I'm a bit of a daredevil myself and I'd really like to give one a try. It would be so much more dignified than having to call for the fire brigade.

L8ers,
   Buzz

Dear Santa,

Are butterflies really just bits of tissue paper that have learnt to fly?

Wilkins

Dear Santa,

Whenever my owner carries anything electrical around the house, he always makes a point of `inadvertently` trailing the power lead behind him. I'm sure he's doing it on purpose – he knows I can't just let a thing like that go. And if he thinks I can't see him smirking he's deluding himself. I've heard there are organizations that clamp down on this sort of treatment.

Can you put me in touch?

Mog

Dear Santa,
Christmas is a time for remembering other cats less fortunate than ourselves. Unfortunately, I don't really have time for all that. Could you take care of it?

Most kind,
Hilton

Dear Santa,

I'd really like to be a tiger, just for a day. Please could you bring me a tiger suit? I'm a size 4.

Grrrrr,
Sid

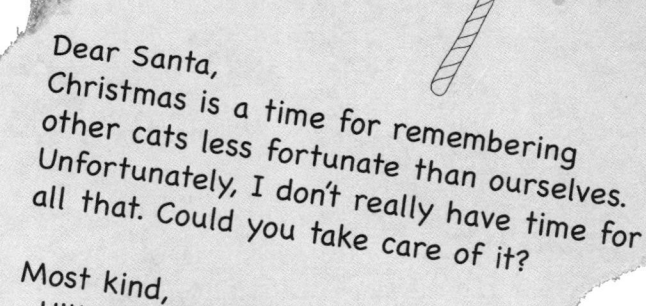

G'day Santa,

My mate Bruce has got me worried. He reckons that because it's the middle of summer here and all the people are wandering about in thongs and cossies, you'll give us a miss with the pressies. He says you only go places with snow and shepherds washing their socks by night. Is that true? Seems a bit harsh to me.

Shane, Adelaide

Dear Santa,

When I close my eyes I dream of a place that's always warm, with a roaring log fire and thick, velvet curtains I can run up and down. There's a live fish swimming around in my food bowl, a ball of wool always dangling just out of reach and a team of tame dogs who massage me and sing me barber's shop versions of Nat King Cole songs. It's funny, I've been having the same dream ever since they varnished the kitchen floor.

Have a cool Christmas,

Jaz

Dear Santa,

Spare a thought for those of us who can't be with our loved ones at this time of year. My family will be celebrating Christmas on the farm as they always do, around the fire with songs and games and lots of lovely things to eat. Alas, I can't be with them, since the little girl came and took me away. I guess that's the price you pay for being cute.

Sniff,
    Lucy

Dear Santa,

When you pull up outside this Christmas, please can you ask your reindeer to keep the noise down? The sound of jingle bells always wakes me up and sends me running to the chimney, thinking it's my ball.

Gratefully,
  Manuel

PS: They lost my ball
two years ago.

Dear Santa,

It's not that I don't appreciate the people in this house, but I'd be really grateful if you can encourage them to take a trip away over Christmas, just so I can have the run of the house for a day or two. I've figured out how to hold open the cat flap so anyone can get in, and Killer says he can get hold of some catnip. Party time!

Our secret though, right?
   Tabs

Dear Santa,

Do they make wetsuits for cats? My owner's been talking about taking me surfing. I'm not mad keen; I could happily go through life without knowing the thrill of shooting the tube or hanging ten, but he's told me there could be fish involved.

Dude

Dear Santa,

So they want me to do my predatory thing with any rats I come across but I'm not allowed to go near the hamster.

Can you explain the difference?

Nikita

Dear Santa,

The little boy I play with has asked for a train set for Christmas. What use is a train set to a girl like me? Please don't bring him a train set. Bring him another ball of wool.

Dolly

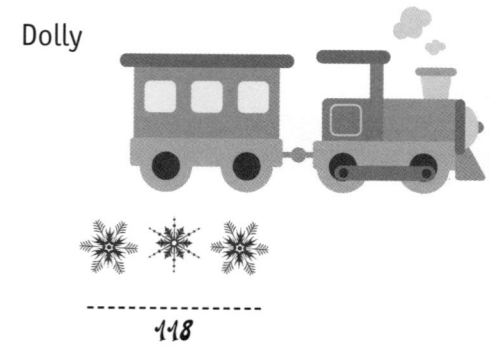

Dear Santa,

What would you like to have been if you hadn't become Santa? I think I'd like to have been a tortoise. Now there's an animal that knows how to relax! You can be talking to our tortoise and you suddenly realize he dropped off three weeks ago and hasn't listened to a word you've said. Hah! I'd really love a camera so I can take a picture of him when he wakes up. I like to flip him on his back so that when he first pokes his head out he thinks he's hanging from the ceiling. You should see his face — it's priceless.

Love and goodwill,
Simpkins

Dear Santa,

Can you tell me, what's the average life expectancy of a dog? And a cat?

Kind regards,

Maisie

Dear Santa,

I'd be very grateful if you could see your way clear to giving me a miner's lamp. You know, one of those ones you strap to your head so it lights your passage under the floorboards. I don't know what they've been putting in my food, but my night vision just ain't what it used to be. Last time I went mousing I cracked my skull on a gas pipe and had to endure ribald laughter from unseen rodents for days. It's just not dignified.

Yours pleadingly,
Killer

Dear Santa,

All I ask for this Christmas is peace on Earth. The world is full of shouting and fighting, everyone putting themselves first and nobody listening to others. It makes it terribly hard to sleep.

Wearily,
 Lord Fluffikins

Dear Santa,

This Christmas I would like a bubble machine. I think my owners are getting tired of the old jumping for the dangly bathroom lightswitch routine.

Lots of love,
 Tiddles

Dear Santa,

Be careful as you come down the chimney.
The staff have put holly in the grate to
stop me using it as a toilet.

Warm regards,
  Trevor

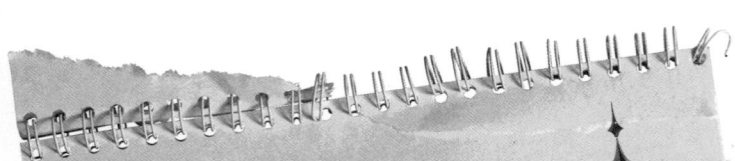

Dear Santa,

Can you perform some miracle that will get my owner to oil the hinges on the garden gate? Every time it opens it squeaks like a mouse and it's playing havoc with my nerves. I can't spend my entire life in 'pounce' mode.

Brompton

Dear Santa,

Last time you came there were four humans in my house. This time you'll find there are five. (I know – like rabbits.) I don't mind babies, but with me that makes six. You know as well as I do that six is a very unlucky number. One of us has to go. Either that or we get some white heather. Do you have any heather?

Myrtle

Dear Santa,

For Christmas I would like a leaf. I love leaves. I like the funny way they dance when they're falling from the sky. But there don't seem to be any around any more. Please bring me a leaf.

Thank you,

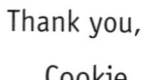

Cookie

Dear Santa,

Please can you bring me the recipe for Raw Turkey? She made it for me last Christmas but hasn't had another go since. If you can have it neatly typed up in quite large print (her eyesight's going as well as her memory), I can leave it on her pillow Christmas morning.

Thank you,

Petra